EASY HITS PIANO EDITION

Alfred's
Easy piano songs

STANDARDS & JAZZ

50 CLASSICS FROM THE GREAT AMERICAN SONGBOOK

Produced by
Alfred Music
P.O. Box 10003
Van Nuys, CA 91410-0003
alfred.com

Printed in USA.

ISBN-10: 1-4706-3292-6
ISBN-13: 978-1-4706-3292-2

Cover Photos
Black piano © iStock.com/The AYS

contents

AIN'T MISBEHAVIN'

Words by
ANDY RAZAF

Music by
THOMAS "FATS" WALLER
and HARRY BROOKS

Moderate swing (♩ = 92)

(with pedal)

Refrain:

No one to talk with, all by my-self. No one to walk with, but I'm hap-py on___ the shelf.

Ain't mis-be-hav-in', I'm sav-in' my love for you.

I know for cer-tain the one I love. I'm through with flirt-in', it's just you I'm think-in' of.

Ain't Misbehavin' - 2 - 1

C A7 Dm G7 C F C E7
Ain't mis-be-hav-in', I'm sav-in' my love for you.
Am F7/A D7/A A7
Like Jack Hor-ner in the cor-ner, don't go no-where; what do I care.
G/D G♯dim7 Am7 D7 G7 A7 D7 G7 C C♯dim7
Your kiss-es are worth wait-in' for, be-lieve me. I don't stay out late,
Dm7 G7 C Gm7 C7 F B♭7 C A7
don't care to go. I'm home a-bout eight, just me and my ra-di-o. Ain't mis-be-hav-in',
1. 2.
Dm G7 C A7 D7 G7 C N.C. C
I'm sav-in' my love for you. you.

AT LAST

Lyrics by
MACK GORDON

Music by
HARRY WARREN

At Last - 3 - 1

ALL OF ME

Words and Music by
GERALD MARKS and
SEYMOUR SIMONS

All of Me - 2 - 1

BLUE MOON

Lyrics by
LORENZ HART

Music by
RICHARD RODGERS

for; you heard me say-ing a pray'r___ for

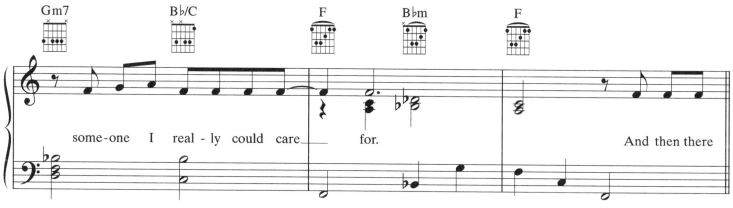

some-one I real-ly could care___ for. And then there

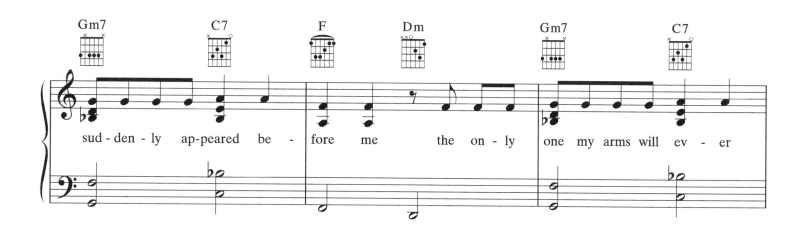

sud-den-ly ap-peared be - fore me the on - ly one my arms will ev - er

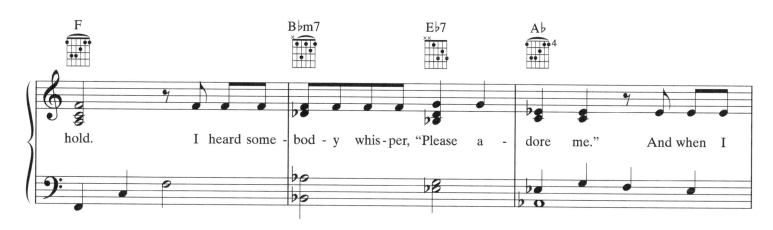

hold. I heard some-bod-y whis-per, "Please a - dore me." And when I

BREEZIN'

Words and Music by
BOBBY WOMACK

Moderately, with a half-time feel ($\quarternote$ = 160) ($\halfnote$ = 80)

Breezin' - 3 - 1

CARAVAN

Words by
IRVING MILLS

Music by
DUKE ELLINGTON and JUAN TIZOL

Caravan - 3 - 1

DO NOTHIN' TILL YOU HEAR FROM ME

Lyric by
BOB RUSSELL

Music by
DUKE ELLINGTON

DON'T GET AROUND MUCH ANYMORE

Lyrics by
BOB RUSSELL

Music by
DUKE ELLINGTON

Don't Get Around Much Anymore - 2 - 1

EMILY

Words by
JOHNNY MERCER

Music by
JOHNNY MANDEL

Em - i - ly, Em - i - ly, Em - i - ly_____ has the

mur - mur - ing sound of May. All

sil - ver bells, cor - al shells, car - ou - sels,_____ and the

Emily - 3 - 1

FIVE FOOT TWO, EYES OF BLUE

Lyrics by
SAM LEWIS and JOE YOUNG

Music by
RAY HENDERSON

Moderately bright two-beat style (♩ = 132)

Refrain:

Five foot two, eyes of blue, but oh, what those five foot can do! Has an-y-bod-y seen my girl?

GENTLE RAIN

Words by
MATT DUBEY

Music by
LUIZ BONFA

GOOD MORNING, HEARTACHE

Words and Music by
ERVIN DRAKE, DAN FISHER
and IRENE HIGGINBOTHAM

I'M IN THE MOOD FOR LOVE

Lyrics by
DOROTHY FIELDS

Music by
JIMMY McHUGH

Moderately (♩ = 92)

(with pedal)

Refrain:

I'm in the mood for love

sim-ply be-cause you're near me. Fun-ny, but when you're

near me, I'm in the mood for love.

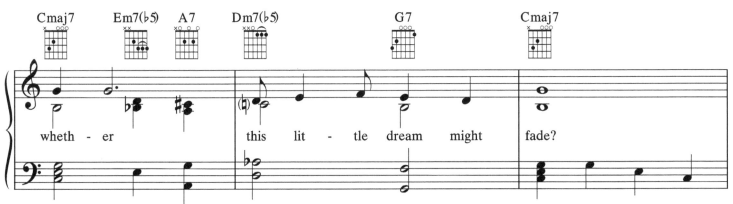

HERE'S THAT RAINY DAY

Words by
JOHNNY BURKE

Music by
JAMES VAN HEUSEN

IN A SENTIMENTAL MOOD

Lyrics by
IRVING MILLS and MANNY KURTZ

Music by
DUKE ELLINGTON

In a Sentimental Mood - 3 - 1

IN YOUR OWN SWEET WAY

By DAVE BRUBECK

In Your Own Sweet Way - 3 - 1

INVITATION

Lyrics by
PAUL FRANCIS WEBSTER

Music by
BRONISLAU KAPER

You and your smile____ hold a strange in - vi - ta - tion.____ Some-how it

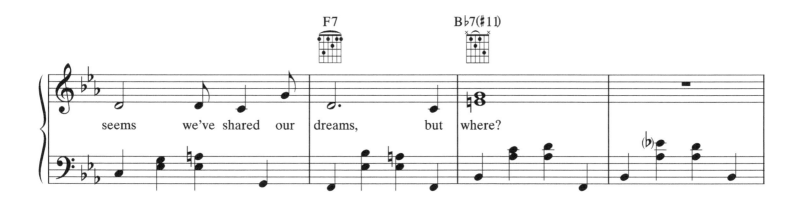

seems we've shared our dreams, but where?

Time af - ter time____ in a room full of strang - ers,____ out of the

Invitation - 3 - 1

IT DON'T MEAN A THING
(If It Ain't Got That Swing)

Words by
IRVING MILLS

Music by
DUKE ELLINGTON

It Don't Mean a Thing - 3 - 1

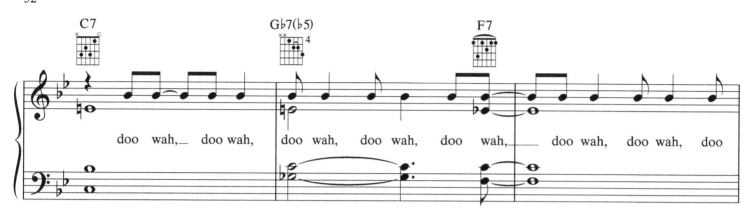

doo wah,___ doo wah, doo wah, doo wah, doo wah,___ doo wah, doo wah, doo

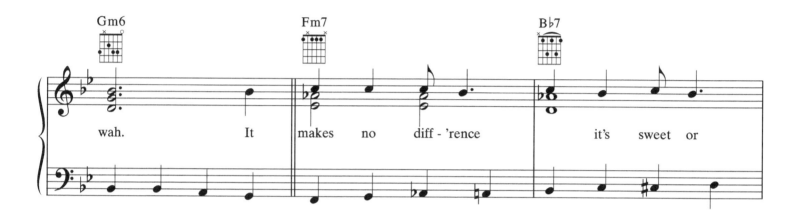

wah. It makes no diff - 'rence it's sweet or

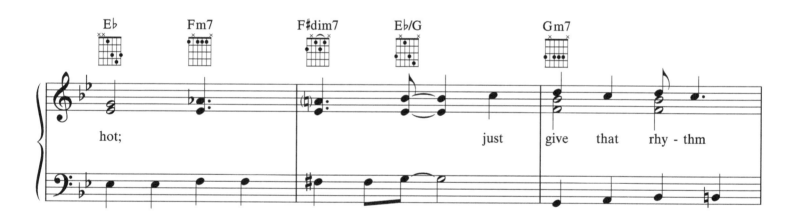

hot; just give that rhy - thm

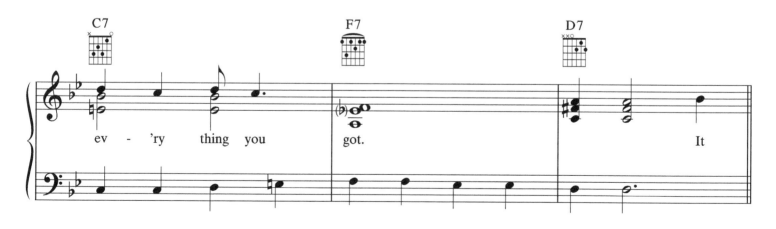

ev - 'ry thing you got. It

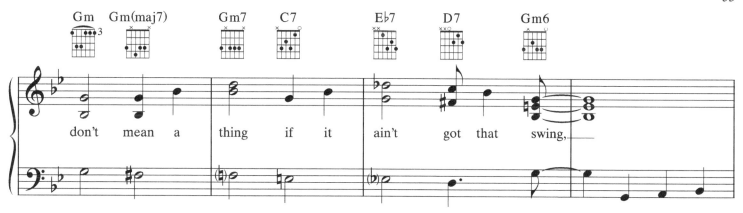

don't mean a thing if it ain't got that swing,

doo wah,___ doo wah, doo wah, doo wah, doo wah,___ doo wah, doo wah, doo

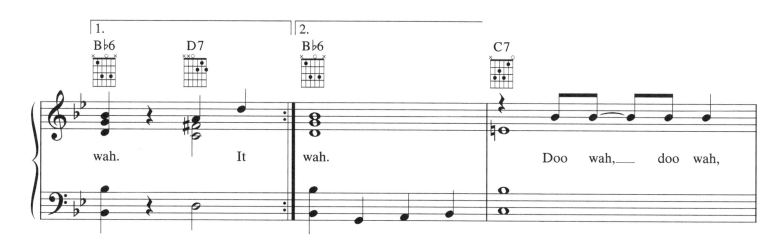

wah. It wah. Doo wah,___ doo wah,

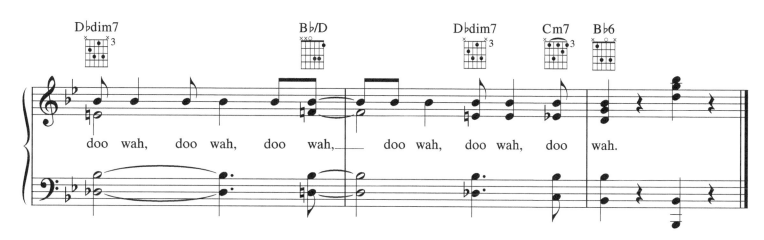

doo wah, doo wah, doo wah,___ doo wah, doo wah, doo wah.

It Don't Mean a Thing - 3 - 3

JUST FRIENDS

Lyrics by
SAM M. LEWIS

Music by
JOHN KLENNER

LAURA

Lyrics by
JOHNNY MERCER

Music by
DAVID RAKSIN

Laura - 2 - 1

LUSH LIFE

By BILLY STRAYHORN

Slow ballad (♩ = 63)

Refrain:

MISTY

Words by
JOHNNY BURKE

Music by
ERROLL GARNER

Misty - 3 - 1

MOONGLOW

Words and Music by
WILL HUDSON, EDDIE DeLANGE
and IRVING MILLS

MOONLIGHT IN VERMONT

Lyric by
JOHN BLACKBURN

Music by
KARL SUESSDORF

Moonlight in Vermont - 3 - 1

MOONLIGHT SERENADE

Lyrics by
MITCHELL PARISH

Music by
GLENN MILLER

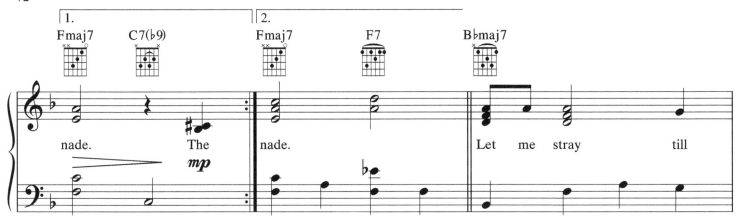

nade. The nade. Let me stray till

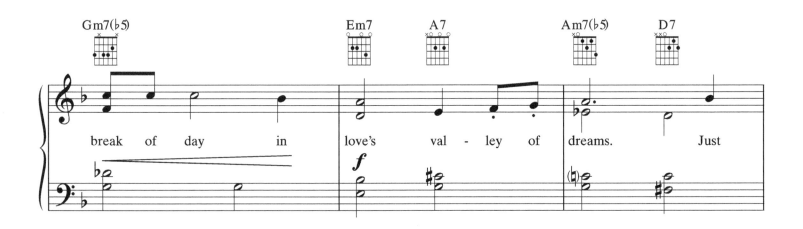

break of day in love's val - ley of dreams. Just

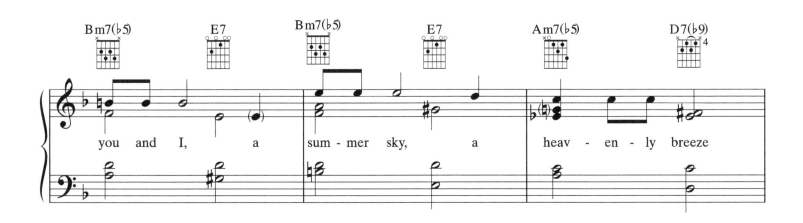

you and I, a sum - mer sky, a heav - en - ly breeze

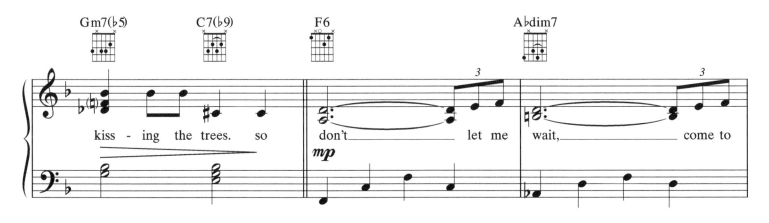

kiss - ing the trees. so don't_____ let me wait,_____ come to

MORE THAN YOU KNOW

Words by
WILLIAM ROSE and EDWARD ELISCU

Music by
VINCENT YOUMANS

MY FOOLISH HEART

Words by
NED WASHINGTON

Music by
VICTOR YOUNG

NICE 'N' EASY

Lyrics by
ALAN and MARILYN BERGMAN

Music by
LEW SPENCE

Nice 'n' Easy - 3 - 1

ON GREEN DOLPHIN STREET

Lyrics by
NED WASHINGTON

Music by
BRONISLAU KAPER

OVER THE RAINBOW

(from *The Wizard of Oz*)

Lyrics by
E.Y. HARBURG

Music by
HAROLD ARLEN

Some - where o - ver the rain - bow, way up high,

there's a land that I heard of once in a lull - a - by.

Some - where o - ver the rain - bow skies are blue,

Over the Rainbow - 3 - 1

POLKA DOTS AND MOONBEAMS

Words by
JOHNNY BURKE

Music by
JIMMY VAN HEUSEN

THEME FROM *NEW YORK, NEW YORK*

Words by
FRED EBB

Music by
JOHN KANDER

PRELUDE TO A KISS

Words by
IRVING MILLS and IRVING GORDON

Music by
DUKE ELLINGTON

SATIN DOLL

Words and Music by
JOHNNY MERCER, DUKE ELLINGTON
and BILLY STRAYHORN

Satin Doll - 3 - 1

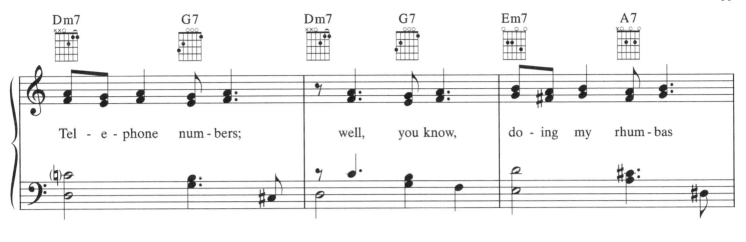

Tel - e - phone num - bers; well, you know, do - ing my rhum - bas

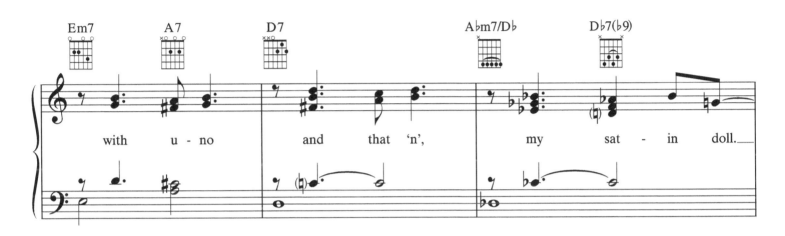

with u - no and that 'n', my sat - in doll.

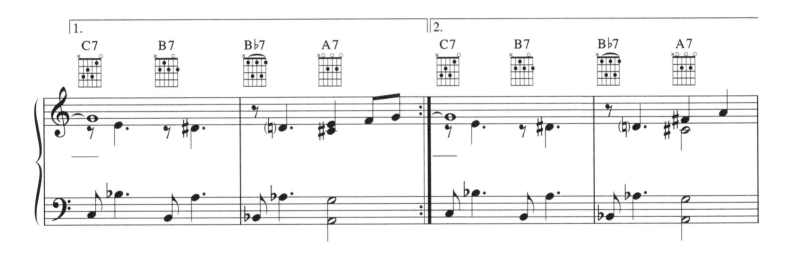

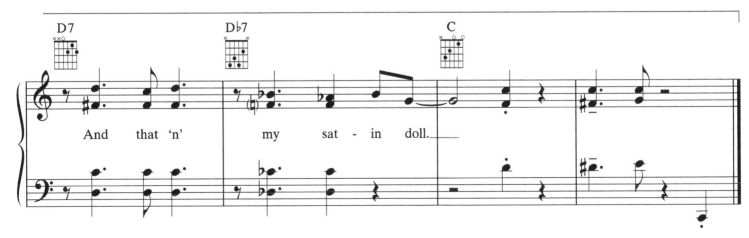

And that 'n' my sat - in doll.

THE SHADOW OF YOUR SMILE

(from *The Sandpiper*)

Lyrics by
PAUL FRANCIS WEBSTER

Music by
JOHNNY MANDEL

The Shadow of Your Smile - 2 - 1

SOFTLY, AS I LEAVE YOU

English Lyric by
HAL SHAPER

Music by
ANTONIO DEVITA

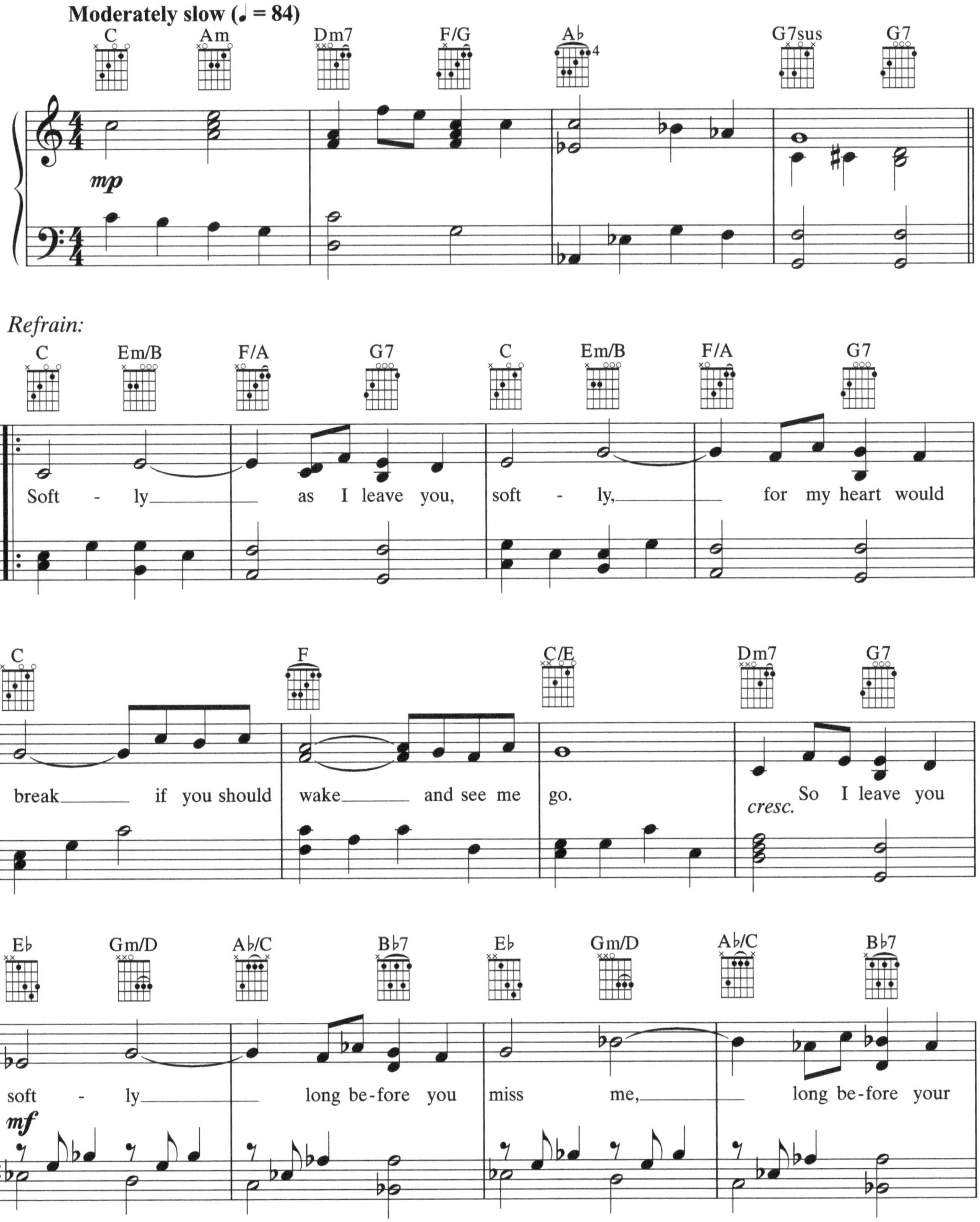

Moderately slow (♩ = 84)

Refrain:

Soft - ly_____ as I leave you, soft - ly,_____ for my heart would break_____ if you should wake_____ and see me go. *cresc.* So I leave you soft - ly_____ long be-fore you miss me, long be-fore your

Softly, as I Leave You - 2 - 1

SOLITUDE

By DUKE ELLINGTON,
EDDIE DeLANGE and IRVING MILLS

STARDUST

Words by
MITCHELL PARISH

Music by
HOAGY CARMICHAEL

Stardust - 2 - 1

STARS FELL ON ALABAMA

Lyric by
MITCHELL PARISH

Music by
FRANK PERKINS

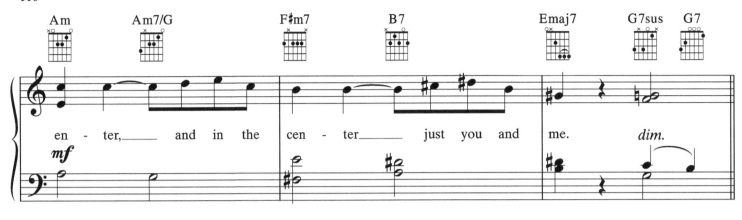

en - ter,_____ and in the cen - ter_____ just you and me. *dim.*

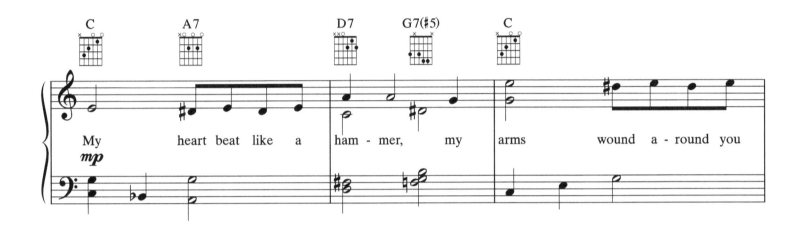

My heart beat like a ham - mer, my arms wound a - round you

tight, and stars fell on Al - a - bam - a last

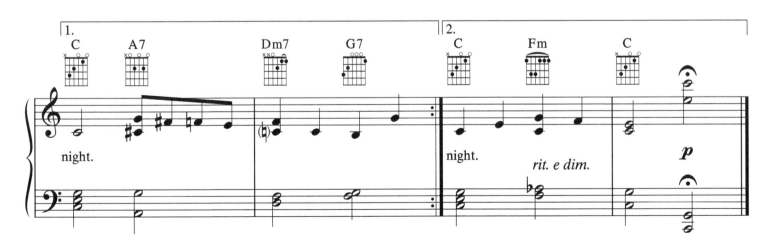

night. night. *rit. e dim.*

STOMPIN' AT THE SAVOY

Lyrics by
ANDY RAZAF

Music by
BENNY GOODMAN, EDGAR SAMPSON
and CHICK WEBB

Easy swing (♩ = 96) (♫ = ♩³♪)

Sa - voy, the home of sweet ro - mance, Sa - voy, it wins you at a glance.

Sa - voy gives hap - py feet a chance to dance.

Your form, just like a cling - ing vine,

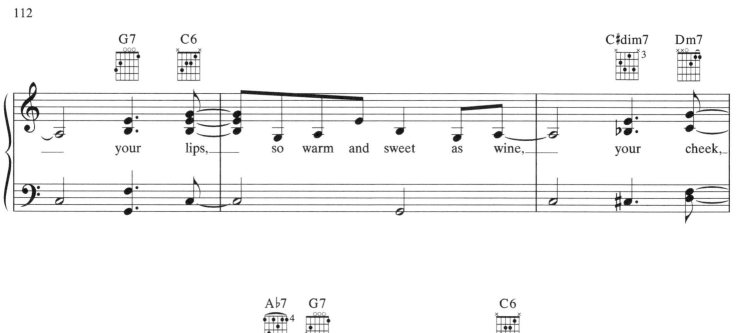

your lips,_____ so warm and sweet as wine,_____ your cheek,

_____ so soft and close to mine,_____ di - vine._____

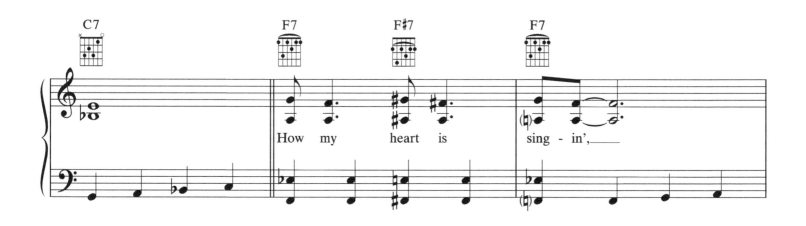

How my heart is sing - in',_____

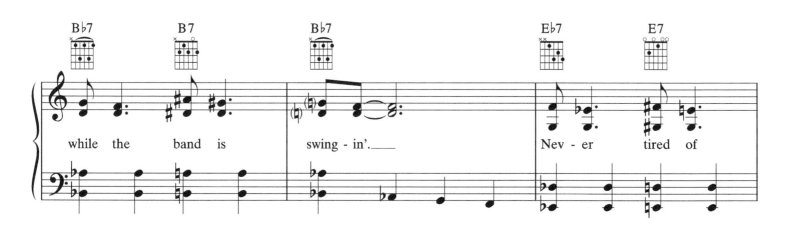

while the band is swing - in'._____ Nev - er tired of

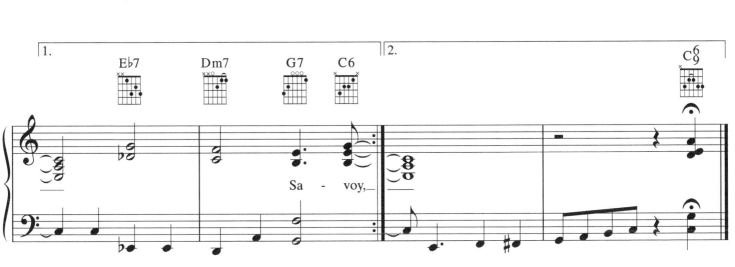

STRAIGHTEN UP AND FLY RIGHT

Moderate swing (♩ = 112) (♫ = ♪³♪)

Words and Music by
NAT KING COLE and IRVING MILLS

Verse:

buz-zard took a mon-key for a ride in the air, the mon-key thought that ev-'ry-thing was on the square.__ The buz-zard tried to throw the mon-key off his back__ but the mon-key turned a-round and said, "Now lis-ten, Jack!"__

Straighten Up and Fly Right - 3 - 1

STREET OF DREAMS

Words and Music by
SAM M. LEWIS and VICTOR YOUNG

Slowly, freely (♩ = 80)

Verse:

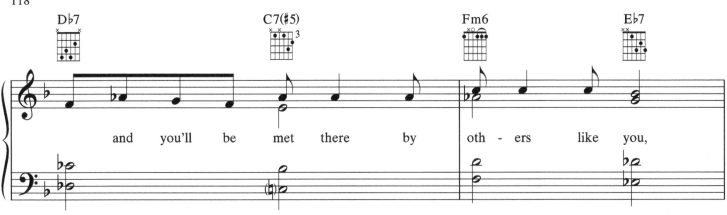

and you'll be met there by oth - ers like you,

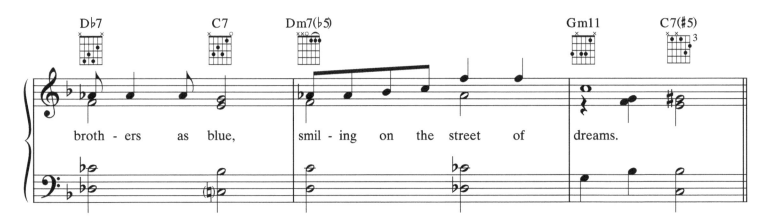

broth - ers as blue, smil - ing on the street of dreams.

Easy swing ($\quarternote$ = 80) ($\eighthnote\eighthnote$ = $\overset{3}{\triplet}$)
Refrain:

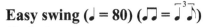

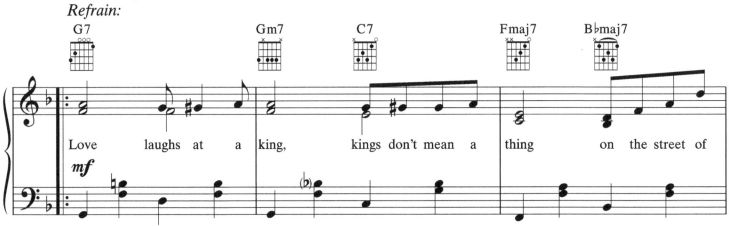

Love laughs at a king, kings don't mean a thing on the street of

mf

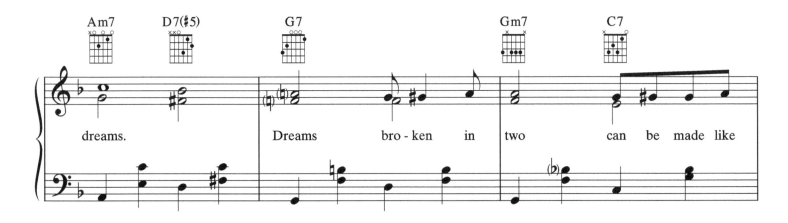

dreams. Dreams bro - ken in two can be made like

TAKE FIVE

By PAUL DESMOND

Take Five - 3 - 2

D.S 𝄋 *al Coda*   𝄌 *Coda*

TAKE THE "A" TRAIN

Words and Music by
BILLY STRAYHORN

Moderately bright swing (♩ = 132) (♫ = ♪³♪)

Refrain:

You must take the "A" train to go to Sug-ar Hill way up in Har-lem.

THIS MASQUERADE

Words and Music by
LEON RUSSELL

This Masquerade - 4 - 1

TRY A LITTLE TENDERNESS

Words and Music by
HARRY WOODS, JIMMY CAMPBELL
and REG CONNELLY

ness. It's not just sen-ti-men-tal,

she has her grief and her care. And a word____ that's soft and gen-tle, makes it

eas-i-er to bear. You won't re-gret it, wom-en don't for-get it,

love is their whole hap-pi-ness. It's all so eas-y, try a lit-tle ten-der-

1. ness.

2. ness.

WHAT'S NEW?

Lyrics by
JOHNNY BURKE

Music by
BOB HAGGART

(with pedal)

What's New? - 3 - 1

WHAT ARE YOU DOING
THE REST OF YOUR LIFE?

Lyrics by
ALAN and MARILYN BERGMAN

Music by
MICHEL LEGRAND

YOU MUST BELIEVE IN SPRING

Lyrics by
ALAN and MARILYN BERGMAN

Music by
MICHEL LEGRAND

When lone-ly feel-ings chill the mea-dows of your mind,
just think when win-ter comes, can spring be far be-hind?
Be-neath the deep-est snows, the se-cret of a rose

You Must Believe in Spring - 3 - 1

YOU STEPPED OUT OF A DREAM

Lyrics by
GUS KAHN

Music by
NACIO HERB BROWN